THE IROQUOIS

A TRUE BOOK®

by

Stefanie Takacs

Children's Press®
A Division of Scholastic Inc.

New York Toronto London Auckland Sydney
Mexico City New Delhi Hong Kong
Danbury, Connecticut

A Mohawk grandmother and granddaughter looking at family photos

Reading Consultant
Jeanne Clidas, Ph.D.
*National Reading Consultant
and Professor of Reading,
SUNY Brockport*

Content Consultant
Neal B. Keating, Ph.D.
*Assistant Professor
of Religious Studies
Hamilton College*

The photo on the cover shows a Tuscarora man doing a traditional dance. The photo on the title page shows Mohawk boys canoeing on the Kahnawake Reserve in Canada.

Library of Congress Cataloging-in-Publication Data

Takacs, Stefanie.
    The Iroquois / by Stefanie Takacs—1st American ed.
        p. cm. — (A true book)
    Includes bibliographical references and index.
Contents: The Iroquois Confederacy—Leadership—Daily life—Housing
and food—The arrival of Europeans—The Haudenosaunee today.
    ISBN 0-516-22777-7 (lib. bdg.)   0-516-27824-X (pbk.)
    1. Iroquois Indians—Juvenile literature. [1. Iroquois Indians. 2. Indians
of North America—New York (State)] I. Title. II. Series.
E99.I7T295 2003
974.7004'9755—dc21

                                                                    2003004540

1 2 3 4 5 6 7 8 9 10 R 12 11 10 09 08 07 06 05 04 03

Contents

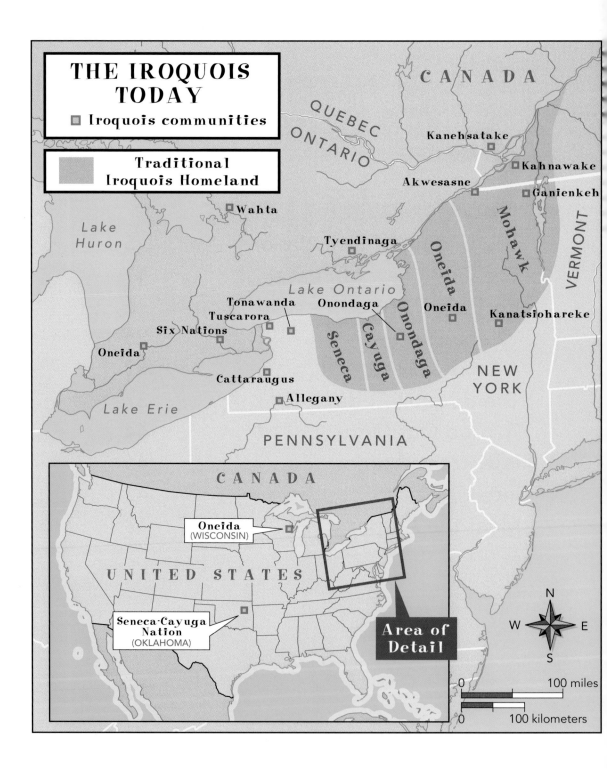

THE IROQUOIS TODAY

□ Iroquois communities

Traditional Iroquois Homeland

CANADA

QUEBEC

ONTARIO

Kanehsatake

Kahnawake

Akwesasne

Ganienkeh

Wahta

VERMONT

Tyendinaga

Mohawk

Lake Huron

Oneida

Lake Ontario

Tonawanda

Onondaga

Oneida

Tuscarora

Onondaga

Oneida

Kanatsiohareke

Six Nations

Seneca

Cayuga

Oneida

Cattaraugus

NEW YORK

Allegany

Lake Erie

PENNSYLVANIA

CANADA

Oneida
(WISCONSIN)

UNITED STATES

Seneca-Cayuga
Nation
(OKLAHOMA)

Area of
Detail

N
W   E
S

0   100 miles

0   100 kilometers

The Uniting of Five Nations

The Iroquois (EAR-o-koy) **Confederacy** is a group of five American Indian **nations** that joined together sometime between A.D.1400 and 1600. They were the Seneca, the Mohawk, the Oneida (o-NY-da), the Onondaga (o-non-DA-ga), and the Cayuga (ky-U-ga) peoples.

These nations have lived for hundreds of years in the area we now call New York State. They each have their own languages, territories, and **heritages**.

The people in the Iroquois Confederacy, or **League**, call themselves *Haudenosaunee* (Ho-DAY-no-SAU-nee). This means "people of the longhouse." A longhouse was a building where many families lived together under one roof. The longhouse is also a

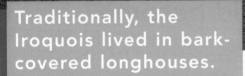

Traditionally, the Iroquois lived in bark-covered longhouses.

symbol for the Iroquois Confederacy.

How the Haudenosaunee became known as the Iroquois is something of a mystery because "Iroquois" is not a name they chose for themselves. It now appears that the name comes

7

from the Basque language, a European language.

Iroquois **oral traditions** say that the League started when a Huron who would become known as the Peacemaker and Hiawatha (hi-a-WA-tha), an Onondaga leader, delivered a message of peace to the five nations. However, it took time for Hiawatha and the Peacemaker to convince the other leaders to work toward peace. Eventually, they all agreed to end the bloodshed

This painting shows Hiawatha and the Peacemaker meeting with an Onondaga medicine man to convince him to stop warring with other nations.

and accept the Great Law of Peace. This started a new relationship of protecting each other from common enemies and extending the Great Law to other nations.

The League of Six Nations

A 1771 British map showing the lands of the League of Six Nations

In 1722, the Iroquois allowed another nation, the Tuscarora, to join them. The British had forced the Tuscarora to flee their home-lands in North Carolina. After the Tuscarora joined the League, the Iroquois were known as the League of Six Nations. The Tuscarora remain today as non-voting members of the Iroquois.

Other Iroquoian peoples were also absorbed into the Confederacy. They lived mostly to the west and southwest of the Iroquois. A number of non-Iroquoian peoples were absorbed into the Confederacy as well, especially during the 1700s.

The Great Law of Peace

When the Iroquois leaders formed the League, their first step was to make the Great Binding Law. This was their constitution, or set of laws. It has about 117 rules. The most important rule is the Great Law of Peace. It says that the people should put an end to

The Iroquois used *wampum*—shell beads—to record important events such as decisions made by the Great Council. The beads were strung into wide belts with patterns representing the event. This 1870s photo shows Iroquois chiefs reading wampum belts.

war and instead settle their differences through peaceful means. The Iroquois still live by the Great Binding Law today.

Important decisions concerning the League were—and still

are—made by the Great Council. It is made up of representatives from each of the five nations. Traditionally, these representatives met at least once a year at the council fire in Onondaga territory. The Onondaga are the keepers of the council fire.

Each member of the Great Council holds a chiefly title, or office. Thirty-one of these titles belong to the Mohawk, Onondaga, and Seneca nations. These nations are the "elder brothers." The other nineteen titles belong to the Oneida and Cayuga nations. They are called the "younger brothers." Those holding offices are known as *royaaner*, or peace chiefs. Historically, peace chiefs held their positions for life. However, during times of unrest, war chiefs competed with peace chiefs for power.

Traditional decision making in the Iroquois Confederacy is done through **consensus**, meaning that the members of the council talk things through

Paintings from the 1700s showing a Seneca chief (left) and Hendrick, a famous Mohawk chief (right)

until they all can come to an agreement. In the event of a tie, the peace chief with the title *Atodarho*, from the Onondaga Nation, is responsible for the final decision.

Iroquois Culture

Equality and sharing are two of the most important **values** in Iroquois society. These values are expressed within large family groups, or clans. The Mohawk and Oneida nations each have three clans: the turtle, bear, and wolf. The Seneca and Cayuga have those three clans plus five more: the heron,

Iroquois children belong to the same clan as their mother. These young people are members of the Mohawk Bear Clan.

snipe, hawk, beaver, and deer. The Onondaga clans include these eight, plus the eel clan.

A clan mother is in charge of each clan, and she has many responsibilities. Traditionally, it was her job to supervise everything in the longhouse and in the fields. It was also her task to choose her clan's chiefs. She was the only person who could remove a chief from his position if he did not do a good job.

Marilyn John, an Oneida clan mother, poses at the Shakowi Cultural Center in Oneida, New York.

The clan mother was not the only woman with power, however. Although the men built the longhouses and other buildings, the women controlled all the property, land, and crops. After the women in a clan decided where they wanted a field, they told the men where to clear away the rocks and trees. Aside from that, the men took no part in the farming.

The women also had the ability to help make their clans larger. When a woman married, her husband moved in with her clan. All of their children became a part of her clan for life.

While the women worked in the fields, tended to the long-house, and cared for the children, the men hunted or fished. In peaceful times, the men fished in

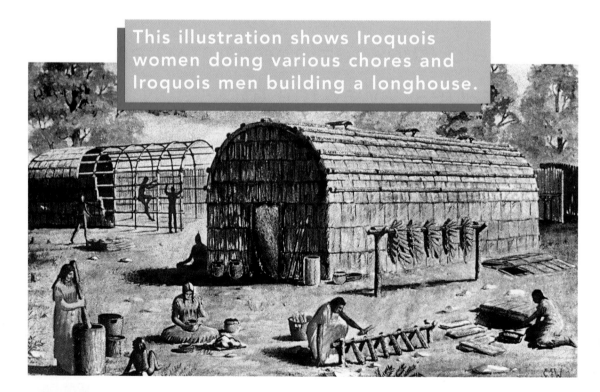

This illustration shows Iroquois women doing various chores and Iroquois men building a longhouse.

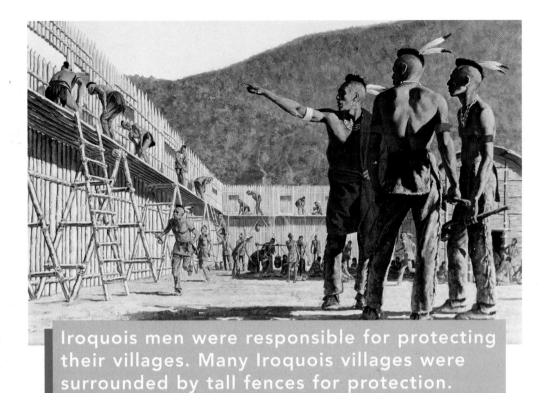

Iroquois men were responsible for protecting their villages. Many Iroquois villages were surrounded by tall fences for protection.

the springtime and hunted in the fall. They left the villages in the autumn to hunt. They did not return with their game until the middle of winter. During times of war, the men protected their villages.

The Iroquois decorated their clothing with beads. At first they used natural materials such as bird bones or seashells. Later, they traded with Europeans for glass beads.

Iroquois people expressed themselves in many different ways. They often painted their

bodies, and also made paintings on trees and bark. Some
images were realistic, while
others were highly abstract.
Before Europeans arrived,
most Iroquois probably
dressed in deerskin clothes,
often adding decorative ele-
ments such as shell jewelry
and feather adornment.

The Iroquois played and
still play a number of sporting
games. The most well-known
game invented by the

Onondaga boys playing lacrosse

Iroquois is lacrosse. It is now played all over the world. Another popular game is snowsnake, a winter game in which players compete to throw a long wooden stick, or "snowsnake," down a long track made in the snow.

gave the families some privacy. In the middle of the longhouse, there were fireplaces for warmth and cooking. Holes in the ceiling of the longhouse allowed the smoke to escape.

   An Iroquois village was made up of from ten to eighty

This is what an Iroquois village in the 1700s might have looked like.

longhouses. Villages were usually relocated about every twenty years for one of two reasons: if the soil was no longer good for farming, or if the village needed better protection from its enemies.

Farming gave the Iroquois their main source of food. In their fields, the women grew crops of corn, beans, and squash. These three crops were known as the Life Supporters or the Three Sisters. Each year, the Iroquois held

The Three Sisters, a sculpture by Mohawk artist Stan Hill, shows the most important crops of the Iroquois: corn, beans, and squash.

several ceremonies of thanksgiving to recognize the gift of life provided by these foods. These ceremonies are still held today.

Hunting and fishing were other important sources of food. The men hunted mostly with bows and arrows. Sometimes they used traps to catch large prey. The Iroquois hunted bear, deer, beavers, rabbits, and muskrats. Deer were the favorite catch. In addition to meat, deer provided hides that could be used for many purposes.

Animal hides and fishing nets hanging inside an Iroquois longhouse

The men fished throughout the year. They used spears and nets to catch their fish. In winter, the Iroquois made holes in the thick lake ice and fished through the holes.

A Look at History

For more than a hundred years, the Iroquois enjoyed a growing society. By the 1600s, there were nearly twenty thousand people in the Iroquois League. About this time, European fur traders landed on the North American continent. These men promised weapons to the Iroquois in return for their furs. The Iroquois

In the 1600s, the Iroquois began trading furs to European traders for metal tools and weapons.

began trading with Europeans in order to absorb them into their Confederacy.

The great demand for fur led the Europeans to trade with many other native peoples. Some of these peoples were the Iroquois's rivals. These enemies now had guns and other weapons. This

In 1609, Frenchman Samuel de Champlain and a group of American Indian rivals of the Iroquois attacked the Mohawk using a weapon they had never seen—the gun.

caused an increase in conflicts between the Iroquois and other native peoples, as well as with Europeans.

Many thousands of Iroquois died because of the fighting. In addition, diseases carried by the Europeans killed many thousands more. Within eighty years, the Iroquois population dropped from about 25,000 people in 1660 to about 14,000 people in 1740.

Life for the Iroquois grew harder as more people arrived from Europe. The formation of the United States in the late 1700s did not help the Iroquois. The U.S. government wanted the Iroquois land for its own people.

The Iroquois were repeatedly misled and forced to sign dozens of treaties that were used to take their land away. The laws of the United States and Canada did

In 1958, the Tuscarora tried without success to stop a government power company from taking over part of their reservation in New York.

not protect American Indian people. In fact, many laws were made to destroy the Indian peoples and their **cultures**. The Iroquois people lost most of their land. But they did not lose all of it. And they did not go away. They are still here today.

The Iroquois Today

Today, the Iroquois people call parts of the United States and Canada home. Presently, there are about 70,000 people in the Iroquois League. About 30,000 of these members live in the United States, in New York, Wisconsin, and Oklahoma. In Canada, Iroquois people live in Ontario and Quebec. Many

Iroquois people enjoy a modern
lifestyle while keeping their
ancestors' traditions alive.

Some people in the nations
do not consider the Iroquois
League to be part of Canada or
the United States. Instead, they
say that they are members of a

separate Confederacy that is older than either the United States or Canada. These Iroquois still hope to have their land returned to them. They also want their rights as an independent group of people to be respected.

A Mohawk girl at a school in Brooklyn, New York, demonstrates a native dance to her classmates.

Iroquois history and culture is celebrated at the Iroquois Indian Museum in Howes Cave, New York. This photo shows an arrow-making demonstration at the museum.

The Iroquois regularly celebrate their culture and their history. Each year, an annual series of ceremonies and **recitations** are performed in many of the communities and nation territories.

At the heart of Iroquois ceremonies is the celebration of life, and the understanding that everything in the world is connected. Everything in the

Onondaga Faithkeeper Oren Lyons puts finishing touches on his painting *Tree of Peace*.

world has a contribution to make to keep life going and to make the world good. For example, the flowing sap of maple trees leads all the other trees into the springtime. Strawberries lead all of the other fruiting plants into the summer by producing the first fruits. And humans communicate with the skyworld above, and through ceremony send up words of thanks.

To Find Out More

Here are some additional resources to help you learn more about the Iroquois:

 **Books**

Bjornlund, Lydia. **The Iroquois** (Indigenous Peoples of North America). Lucent Books, 2001.

Graymont, Barbara. **The Iroquois.** Chelsea House Publishers, 1989.

Hubbard-Brown, Janet. **The Mohawk Indians.** Chelsea House Publishers, 1993.

Levine, Ellen, **If You Lived with the Iroquois.** Scholastic Trade, 1999.

Sita, Lisa. **Indians of the Northeast: Traditions, History, Legends, and Life.** Gareth Stevens Publishing, 2000.

Sneve, Virginia Driving Hawk. **The Iroquois** (A First Americans Book). Holiday House, 1995.

Snow, Dean. **The Iroquois.** Blackwell Publishers, 1996.

Yue, Charlotte. **The Wigwam and the Longhouse.** Houghton Mifflin Company, 2000.

Organizations and Online Sites

American Museum of Natural History
http://anthro.amnh.org

The American Museum of Natural History has a large collection of Iroquois artifacts including masks, baskets, pipes, and weapons. Photographs of many of these artifacts are available online.

Iroquois History
http://www.tolatsga.org/iro.html

This site has detailed information on the history, culture, and population of the nations that make up the Iroquois Confederacy.

Iroquois Indian Museum
P.O. Box 7
Caverns Road
Howes Cave, NY 12092
http://www.iroquoismuseum.org

The Iroquois Indian Museum features a collection of contemporary Iroquois art and historical artifacts that opens a window on Iroquois society and culture.

The Iroquois Nations of the Northeast
http://www.carnegiemuseums.org/cmnh/exhibits/north-south-east-west/iroquois/index.html

This site, from the Carnegie Museum of Natural History, has lots of information on the history, beliefs, and culture of the Iroquois.

Important Words

ancestors relatives who lived long ago

confederacy group of nations joined together

consensus agreement by everyone

culture customs, language, art, beliefs, and practices of a group of people

heritages histories and traditions handed down from the past

league group of people, teams, or nations

nation group of people who live in a certain area, have a particular way of life, speak the same language, and are organized under a central government

oral traditions stories told aloud that are passed from generation to generation

recitations memorized pieces said aloud

saplings young trees

values ideas that a culture believes are important

Index

47

Meet the Author

Stefanie Takacs has worked in social services, youth education and programming, and educational publishing. She has written numerous educational books on reading-test preparation and Native American peoples. Stefanie holds a bachelor's degree in liberal arts and a master's degree in educational psychology.

Experiencing new cultures is part of Stefanie's life. She has lived in Africa, South America, and the United States. She has also traveled extensively through the United Kingdom and Europe. These days Stefanie can be found in the Bronx, New York, or in the Litchfield Hills of Connecticut, where she enjoys gardening, reading, writing, running, painting and drawing, and being with her family.